DK READERS

Level 2

Dinosaur Dinners
Fire Fighter!
Bugs! Bugs! Bugs!
Slinky, Scaly Snakes!
Animal Hospital
The Little Ballerina
Munching, Crunching, Sniffing,
  and Snooping
The Secret Life of Trees
Winking, Blinking, Wiggling,
  and Waggling
Astronaut: Living in Space
Twisters!
Holiday! Celebration Days
  around the World
The Story of Pocahontas
Horse Show
Survivors: The Night the Titanic Sank
Eruption! The Story of Volcanoes
The Story of Columbus
Journey of a Humpback Whale
Amazing Buildings
Feathers, Flippers, and Feet
Outback Adventure: Australian Vacation
Sniffles, Sneezes, Hiccups, and Coughs
Ice Skating Stars
Let's Go Riding
I Want to Be a Gymnast
Starry Sky
Earth Smart: How to Take Care
  of the Environment

Water Everywhere
Telling Time
A Trip to the Theater
Journey of a Pioneer
Inauguration Day
Emperor Penguins
The Great Migration
Star Wars: Journey Through Space
Star Wars: A Queen's Diary
Star Wars: R2-D2 and Friends
Star Wars: Join the Rebels
Star Wars: Clone Troopers in Action
Star Wars: The Adventures of Han Solo
Star Wars The Clone Wars: Jedi in Training
Star Wars The Clone Wars: Anakin in Action!
Star Wars The Clone Wars: Stand Aside—
  Bounty Hunters!
Star Wars The Clone Wars: Boba Fett: Jedi
  Hunter
WWE: John Cena
Spider-Man: Worst Enemies
Power Rangers: Great Adventures
Pokémon: Meet the Pokémon
Pokémon: Meet Ash!
LEGO® Kingdoms: Defend the Castle
LEGO® Star Wars®: The Phantom Menace
Meet the X-Men
Indiana Jones: Traps and Snares
¡Insectos! en español
¡Bomberos! en español
La Historia de Pocahontas en español

Level 3

Shark Attack!
Beastly Tales
Titanic
Invaders from Outer Space
Movie Magic
Time Traveler
Bermuda Triangle
Tiger Tales
Plants Bite Back!
Zeppelin: The Age of the Airship
Spies
Terror on the Amazon
Disasters at Sea
The Story of Anne Frank
Abraham Lincoln: Lawyer, Leader, Legend
George Washington: Soldier, Hero, President
Extreme Sports
Spiders' Secrets
The Big Dinosaur Dig
Space Heroes: Amazing Astronauts
The Story of Chocolate
School Days Around the World
Polar Bear Alert!
Welcome to China
My First Ballet Show
Ape Adventures
Greek Myths

Amazing Animal Journeys
Spacebusters: The Race to the Moon
Ant Antics
WWE: Triple H
WWE: Undertaker
Star Wars: Star Pilot
Star Wars: I Want to Be a Jedi
Star Wars: The Story of Darth Vader
Star Wars: Yoda in Action
Star Wars: Forces of Darkness
Star Wars: Death Star Battles
Star Wars: Feel the Force!
Star Wars The Clone Wars: Forces of Darkness
Star Wars The Clone Wars: Yoda in Action!
Star Wars The Clone Wars: Jedi Heroes
Marvel Heroes: Amazing Powers
The X-Men School
Pokémon: Explore with Ash and Dawn
Pokémon: Become a Pokémon Trainer
The Invincible Iron Man: Friends and Enemies
Wolverine: Awesome Powers
Abraham Lincoln: Abogado, Líder, Leyenda en
  español
Al Espacio: La Carrera a la Luna
  en español
Fantastic Four: The World's Greatest Superteam
Indiana Jones: Great Escapes

A Note to Parents

DK READERS is a compelling program for beginning readers, designed in conjunction with leading literacy experts, including Dr. Linda Gambrell, Distinguished Professor of Education at Clemson University. Dr. Gambrell has served as President of the National Reading Conference, the College Reading Association, and the International Reading Association.

Beautiful illustrations and superb full-color photographs combine with engaging, easy-to-read stories to offer a fresh approach to each subject in the series. Each DK READER is guaranteed to capture a child's interest while developing his or her reading skills, general knowledge, and love of reading.

The five levels of DK READERS are aimed at different reading abilities, enabling you to choose the books that are exactly right for your child:

Pre-level 1: Learning to read
Level 1: Beginning to read
Level 2: Beginning to read alone
Level 3: Reading alone
Level 4: Proficient readers

The "normal" age at which a child begins to read can be anywhere from three to eight years old. Adult participation through the lower levels is very helpful for providing encouragement, discussing storylines, and sounding out unfamiliar words.

No matter which level you select, you can be sure that you are helping your child learn to read, then read to learn!

DK

LONDON, NEW YORK, MUNICH,
MELBOURNE, and DELHI

Series Editor Deborah Lock
U.S. Editor Shannon Beatty
Designer Vikas Sachdeva
Project Designer Akanksha Gupta
Art Director Martin Wilson
Production Editor Sarah Isle
Jacket Designer Natalie Godwin

Reading Consultant
Linda B. Gambrell, Ph.D.

First American Edition, 2012
12 13 14 15 16 10 9 8 7 6 5 4 3 2 1
001-184580-June 2012
Published in the United States by DK Publishing
375 Hudson Street, New York, New York 10014

DK books are available at special discounts when purchased in bulk
for sales promotions, premiums, fund-raising, or educational use.
For details, contact:
DK Publishing Special Markets
375 Hudson Street
New York, New York 10014
SpecialSales@dk.com

A catalog record for this book is available
from the Library of Congress.

ISBN:978-0-7566-9279-7 (Paperback)
ISBN: 978-0-7566-9280-3 (Hardcover)

Color reproduction by Colourscan, Singapore
Printed and bound in China by L.Rex Printing Co., Ltd.

The publisher would like to thank the following for their kind
permission to reproduce their photographs:

Key: a-above; b-below/bottom; c-center; f-far; l-left; r-right; t-top
2 **Dreamstime.com:** Musat Christian (b). 3 **Getty Images:** Keren
Su / The Image Bank. 4-5 **Getty Images:** Adam Bennie / Vetta. 6
Photolibrary: Régis Cavignaux. 7 **Corbis:** Joe McDonald (b). 8
FLPA: David Hosking (c). 8-9 **Getty Images:** Daryl Balfour. 9
Corbis: Wolfgang Kaehler (c). 10 **Getty Images:** Visuals
Unlimited, Inc. / Joe McDonald / Visuals Unlimited (b). 11 **Corbis:**
Andy Rouse (t). 12 **Getty Images:** Suzi Eszterhas / Minden Pictures
(t). 12-13 **Photolibrary:** Melba Melba. 13 **Getty Images:** Juergen
Ritterbach / Photodisc (t). 15 **Getty Images:** Konrad Wothe /
Minden Pictures. 16-17 **Photolibrary:** Malcolm Schuyl / FLPA.
18-19 **Corbis:** Nigel Pavitt / JA. 20 **Getty Images:** Karen Desjardin
/ Photographer's Choice (b). 21 **Corbis:** Momatiuk - Eastcott (t).
Photolibrary: Keith Levit (b). 22-23 **Corbis:** Martin Harvey. 24
Photolibrary: Frank Stober (b). 25 **Corbis:** Denis-Huot / Hemis.
26-27 **Photolibrary:** Anup Shah. 27 **Corbis:** Jake Warga (c). 28
Alamy Images: Photoshot Holdings Ltd. 29 **Getty Images:** Image
Source (t). 30-31 **Corbis:** Paul Souders.

Jacket images: *Front:* **naturepl.com:** Suzi Eszterhas
All other images © Dorling Kindersley
For further information see: www.dkimages.com

Discover more at
www.dk.com

DK READERS

BEGINNING TO READ ALONE **2**

The Great Migration

Written by Deborah Lock

DK Publishing

The short grass
has dried up and little is left.
It is March and no rains are due.
In the south of
the Serengeti National Park,
northern Tanzania,
huge herds of animals gather.
To survive, they must move on
again to find fresh tall grasses.
They must continue on their
never-ending, circular trip,
which is known as
the Great Migration.

The route

Year after year, migrating animals take a clockwise route through the Serengeti and Masai Mara in East Africa. The huge herds are an amazing sight. Each year they travel about 2,000 miles (3,000 km).

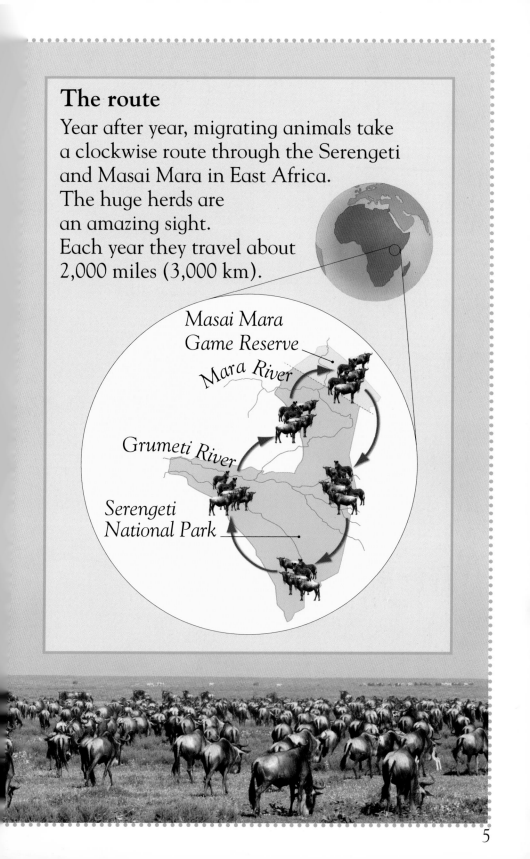

Masai Mara Game Reserve

Mara River

Grumeti River

Serengeti National Park

Masai Mara
Game Reserve

Mara River

Grumeti River

Serengeti
National Park

Since January,
more than a million
wildebeest have grazed on
the Southern Serengeti plains.
Hundreds of thousands of them
have given birth to calves.
The newborn calves stand up
within ten minutes of being born
and stay close to their moms.
There are many dangers.
Hungry hyenas, jackals,
and other hunting
animals attack the
weaker ones for food.

Jackal

Wildebeest grazing

Thousands of gazelles
and zebras also graze
among the wildebeest herds.
They eat different parts of
the grass than the wildebeest.

Serengeti
A large variety of species
of animals and birds lives
in the Serengeti National
Park. With more than four
million animals, this area
has the largest number of
wildlife in the world.

They roam in large numbers so they are safer from attack by meat-eating animals.
By March, they also need to find fresh grass and migrate with the wildebeest.
They head northwest.

Zebras eat the top part of the grass. Wildebeest eat the leaves. Gazelles eat what's left.

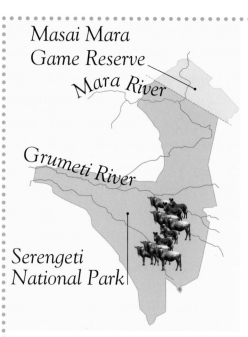

Masai Mara
Game Reserve
Mara River

Grumeti River

Serengeti
National Park

Meat-eating
animals, such
as lions,
hyenas, and
cheetahs, follow
the herds.
They watch for the wildebeest,
gazelles, and zebras that get tired.
They stalk the herds.

If an animal stumbles,
they pounce.
The animal is
too sick or weak
to get up and run.
The hunters kill with
a sharp bite on
the animal's neck.

Scavengers

More than 250,000 wildebeest will die on the journey so there's plenty to eat for scavengers, such as vultures, jackals, and hyenas.

In the air, vultures
watch the herds.
They circle overhead.
When they spot a carcass
of a dead animal, they swoop in.
They rip and tear the meat
from the bones with their beaks.

Hyenas smell
the carcass, too,
and run over to eat.
Vultures hop around
in a frenzy of flapping wings,
trying to get their scraps.

Masai Mara
Game Reserve
Mara River

Grumeti River

Serengeti
National Park

By May,
the herds
have reached
the long grass
plains and
woodlands
in the west of the Serengeti.
The many days of rain
have made these grasses
rich in nutrients.
The animals feast on
the green grass.
For a while, there is plenty
to eat and water to drink.
Then the rains stop.

Male wildebeest stop eating
and fight each other.
These bulls fight for females
and for small areas of land
to impress the females.
They drop onto their front knees,
lower their heads, and lock horns.

They push against each other,
head-to-head.
The grunting sounds
of the fighting bulls
echo around the plains.
The winner is the strongest.

Masai Mara
Game Reserve

Mara River

Grumeti River

Serengeti
National Park

In June, the
huge numbers
of grazing
animals have
eaten all the
good grass.

They move off again,
looking for food and water.
The herds split and head
in different directions.
Some sweep westward,
while others head northward.
Both groups are making
their way to the Masai Mara
Game Reserve in Kenya.
To get there they have to
crisscross the fast-flowing rivers.

Masai Mara
Game Reserve
Mara River

Grumeti River

Serengeti
National Park

In July and August, the migrating animals face their toughest test—the dangerous river crossings. They have been trekking for four months. They are very hungry and very thirsty.

Mara River
The Mara River flows through Kenya and Tanzania to Lake Victoria. Hippos bathe in the river and large Nile crocodiles lurk just below the surface.

By August, they gather
on the banks of the Mara River.
They know that across
the river is food and water.
But the river flows fast,
swollen by the rains.
Also, crocodiles lurk in the water.

The fearful herds grow and grow.
They push and shove.
Who will go first
down the steep bank?
Suddenly, there is
a stampede
as the herds
push forward.

Thousands of wildebeest slip
and slide down the banks
into the river.
They frantically swim across,
battling against
the fast-flowing water.
Calves get separated
from their moms in the chaos.

The river is a swirl of
splashing muddy water.
Some animals are too weak
and are washed away.
Waiting crocodiles snap them up.
The wildebeest surge up
the steep bank on
the other side of the river.
Many stumble and fall back
into the river.

Finally, the strongest reach
the top of the bank and head
for the Masai Mara's plains.

Masai Mara
Game Reserve
Mara River

Grumeti River

Serengeti
National Park

Nearly two million wildebeest, zebras, and gazelles have made it! They settle down to graze with the other animals in the Masai Mara.

The plains are
scattered with
herds of buffalo
and many types of antelope.
Rhinos and giraffes
roam the grasslands.
Baboon troops forage for food.

The Masai tribe
The people living in
the Serengeti and
Masai Mara are called
the Masai. They have
many traditional
customs and look after
cattle, goats, and sheep.

Waterholes are busy places.
The animals and birds have
come to drink.
Families of elephants splash
themselves with water
to cool down.
Lions and cheetahs
watch from a distance,
planning their next hunt.

Hippos bathe
in the rivers,
munching on
the water plants.
Flamingos and
other water
birds flock
to the lakes.

Masai Mara
Game Reserve
Mara River
Grumeti River
Serengeti
National Park

By November, the herds of wildebeest, zebras, and gazelles have stripped the grasslands of the Masai Mara. The rain clouds gather. It is time to move on again.

The animals know they'll find
fresh grass in the Serengeti
where it's also raining.
They head south back to
the Southern Serengeti plains.
There, they will once again
give birth to their calves
early in the new year.

Wildebeest facts

One and a half million wildebeest eat 7,000 tons
of grass a day, which is the same as mowing
more than 100 soccer fields.

Each day, a wildebeest herd drinks enough water
to fill five Olympic-sized swimming pools.

A wildebeest herd produces enough waste
to fill 125 tank trucks and dung to fill
500 dump trucks a day.

In February, 8,000 wildebeest calves are born
each day over three weeks.

Wildebeests are also called gnus
[pronounced NEWS]. They make noisy
low moaning sounds and snort loudly if disturbed.

Index